AULT PUBLIC LIBRARY

3 3455 00 00 6 32

D0772259

DEMCO

E   90303
463.21   14.95

EMBERLEY, REBECCA

My house; a book in two languages

AULT PUBLIC LIBRARY
AULT, COLORADO

My House
A Book in Two Languages

Mi Casa
Un Libro en Dos Lenguas

Rebecca Emberley

This is my house.
Esta es mi casa.
I live here with my family.
Yo vivo aquí con mi familia.
This is my sister's room.
Este es el cuarto de mi hermana.

In simple phrases and bold, colorful images, Rebecca Emberley invites the youngest readers to learn basic words in both Spanish and English. A bilingual treat, just right for children who speak either Spanish or English at home, *My House Mi Casa* makes learning a new language fun and is the perfect way to introduce the very young to the richness of our multicultural society.

E
463.21

My House   Mi Casa

A Book in Two Languages   Un Libro en Dos Lenguas

Rebecca Emberley

Little, Brown and Company
Boston Toronto London

90303
AULT PUBLIC LIBRARY
AULT, COLORADO

Other books by Rebecca Emberley

CITY SOUNDS

JUNGLE SOUNDS

TAKING A WALK/CAMINANDO

DRAWING WITH NUMBERS AND LETTERS

Copyright © 1990 by Rebecca Emberley

All rights reserved. No part of this book may
be reproduced in any form or by any electronic
or mechanical means, including information
storage and retrieval systems, without
permission in writing from the publisher, except
by a reviewer who may quote brief passages
in a review.

First edition

Library of Congress Cataloging-in-Publication Data

Emberley, Rebecca.
     My house = Mi casa : a book in two languages / by Rebecca
Emberley.
          p.   cm.
     Summary: Captioned illustrations and Spanish and English text
describe things found in a house.
     ISBN 0-316-23637-3
     1. Picture dictionaries, Spanish.   2. Picture dictionaries,
English.   3. Spanish language — Glossaries, vocabularies, etc.
4. English language — Glossaries, vocabularies, etc.   5. Dwellings —
Terminology — Juvenile literature.   [1. Vocabulary.   2. Dwellings.
3. Spanish language materials — Bilingual.]   I. Title.   II. Title:
Mi casa.
PC4629.E47   1990
463'.21 — dc20   89-12893
                                                             CIP
                                                              AC

10 9 8 7 6 5 4 3 2 1

WOR

Published simultaneously in Canada by Little,
Brown & Company (Canada) Limited

Printed in the United States of America

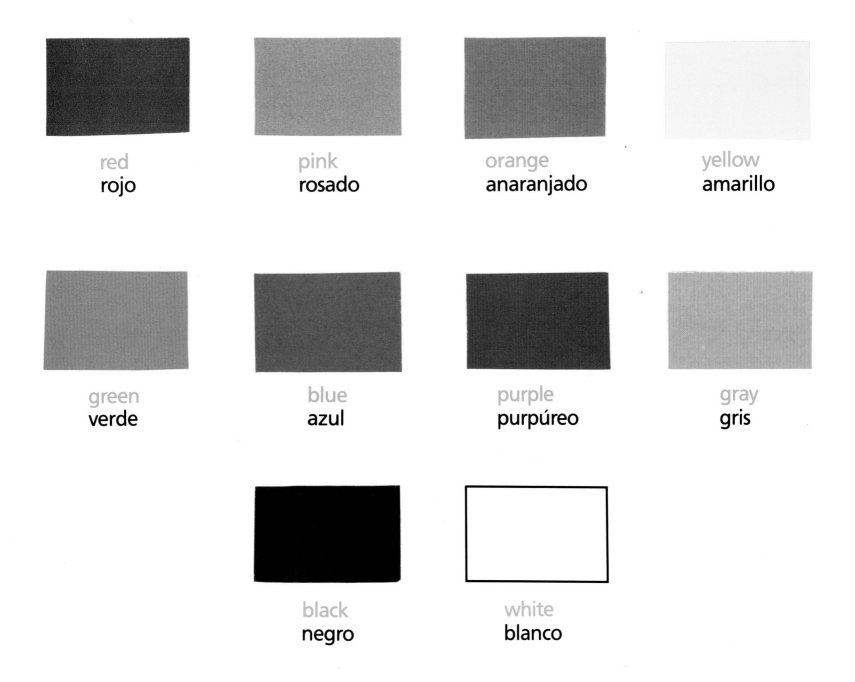

red
rojo

pink
rosado

orange
anaranjado

yellow
amarillo

green
verde

blue
azul

purple
purpúreo

gray
gris

black
negro

white
blanco

Here are some of the colors you will see in this book.
Estos son algunos de los colores que verás en este libro.

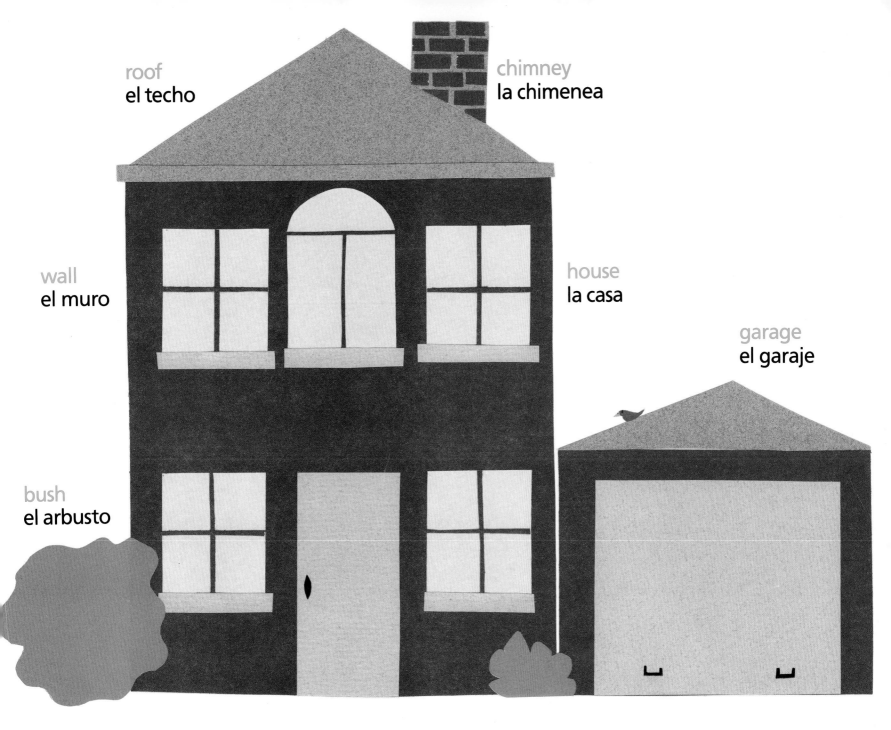

roof
el techo

chimney
la chimenea

wall
el muro

house
la casa

garage
el garaje

bush
el arbusto

This is my house.
Esta es mi casa.

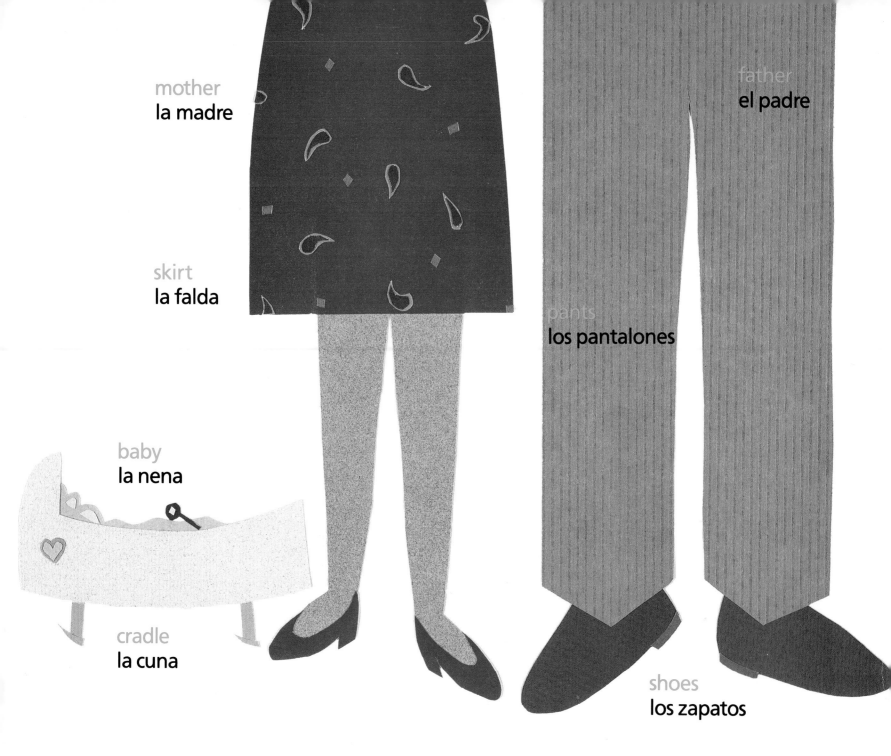

mother
la madre

skirt
la falda

father
el padre

pants
los pantalones

baby
la nena

cradle
la cuna

shoes
los zapatos

I live here with my family
Yo vivo aquí con mi familia

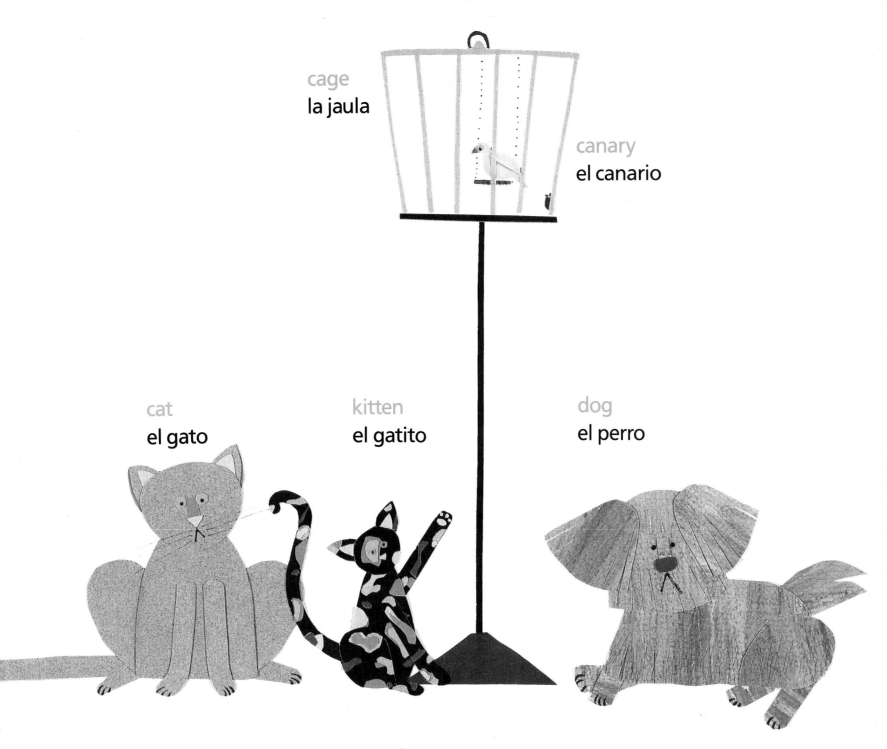

cage
la jaula

canary
el canario

cat
el gato

kitten
el gatito

dog
el perro

and my pets.
y mis mascotas.

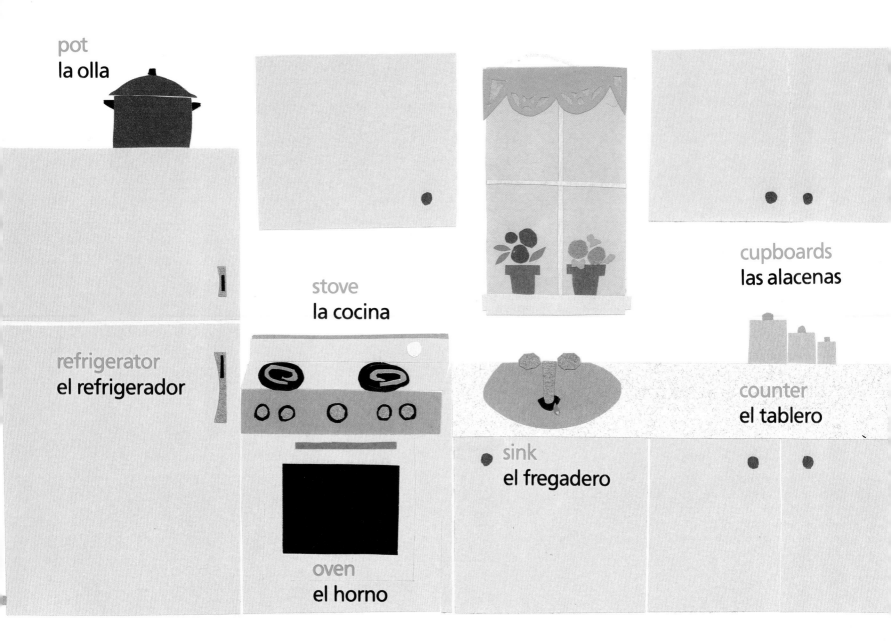

pot
la olla

stove
la cocina

cupboards
las alacenas

refrigerator
el refrigerador

counter
el tablero

sink
el fregadero

oven
el horno

This is the kitchen,
Esta es la cocina,

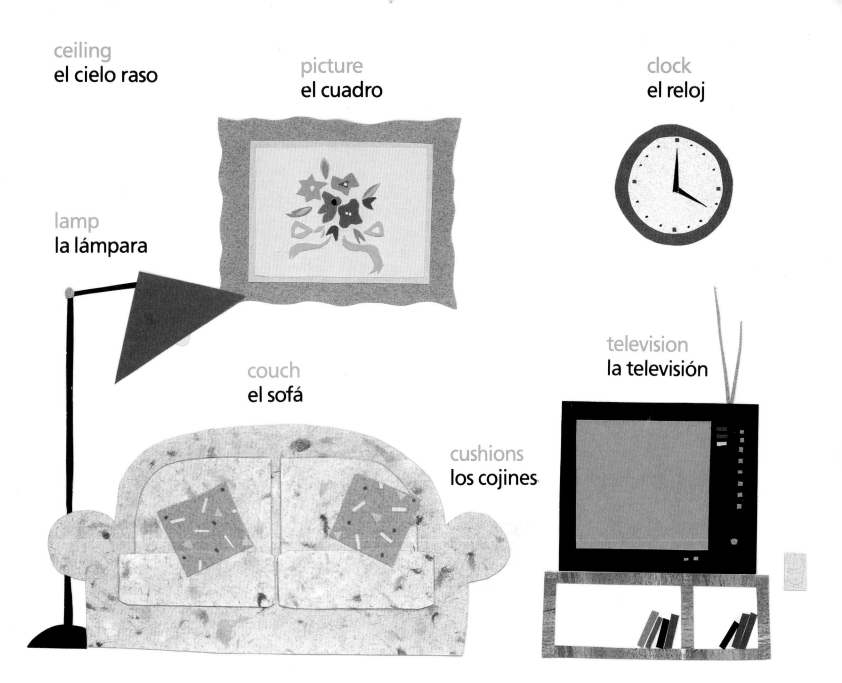

ceiling
el cielo raso

picture
el cuadro

clock
el reloj

lamp
la lámpara

television
la televisión

couch
el sofá

cushions
los cojines

and this is the living room.
y esta es la sala de estar.

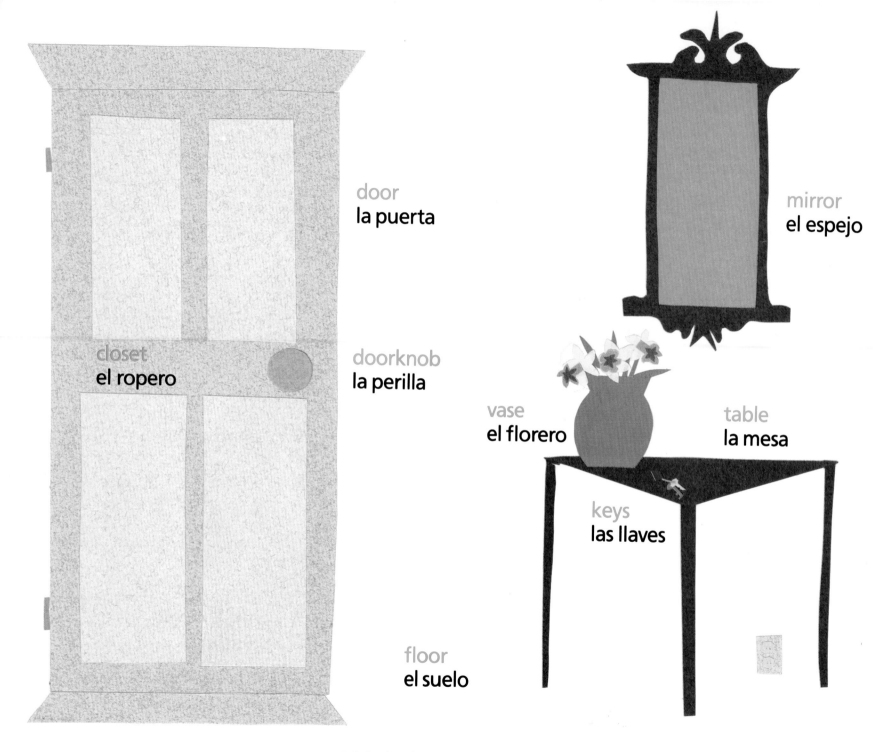

door
la puerta

mirror
el espejo

closet
el ropero

doorknob
la perilla

vase
el florero

table
la mesa

keys
las llaves

floor
el suelo

This is the hallway.
Este es el corredor.

plant
la planta

coatrack
la percha

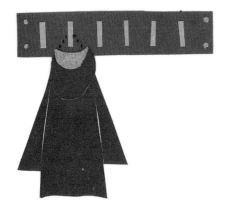

light switch
el apagador de luces

railing
el pasamano

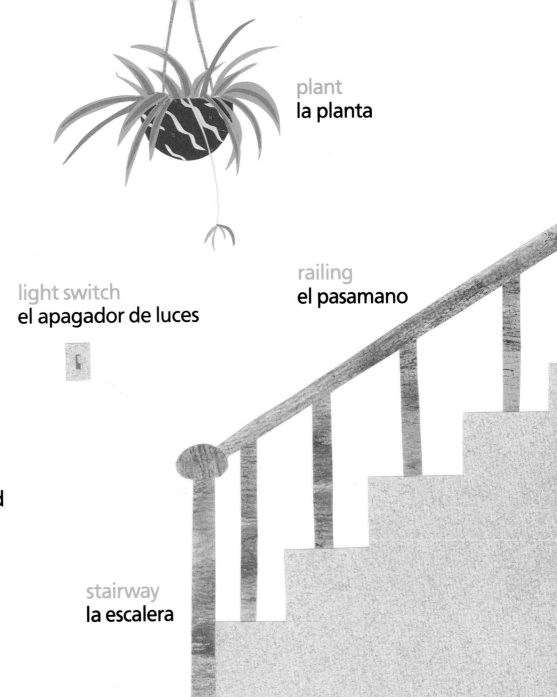

wall
la pared

boots
las botas

stairway
la escalera

Let's go upstairs.
Subamos.

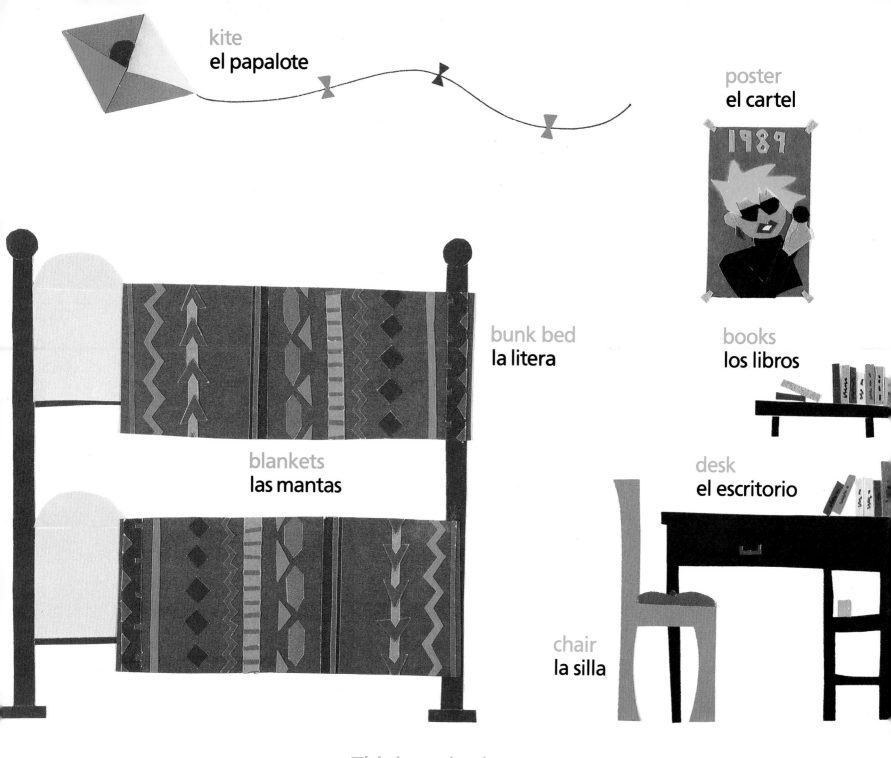

kite
el papalote

poster
el cartel

1989

bunk bed
la litera

books
los libros

blankets
las mantas

desk
el escritorio

chair
la silla

This is my bedroom
Esta es mi alcoba

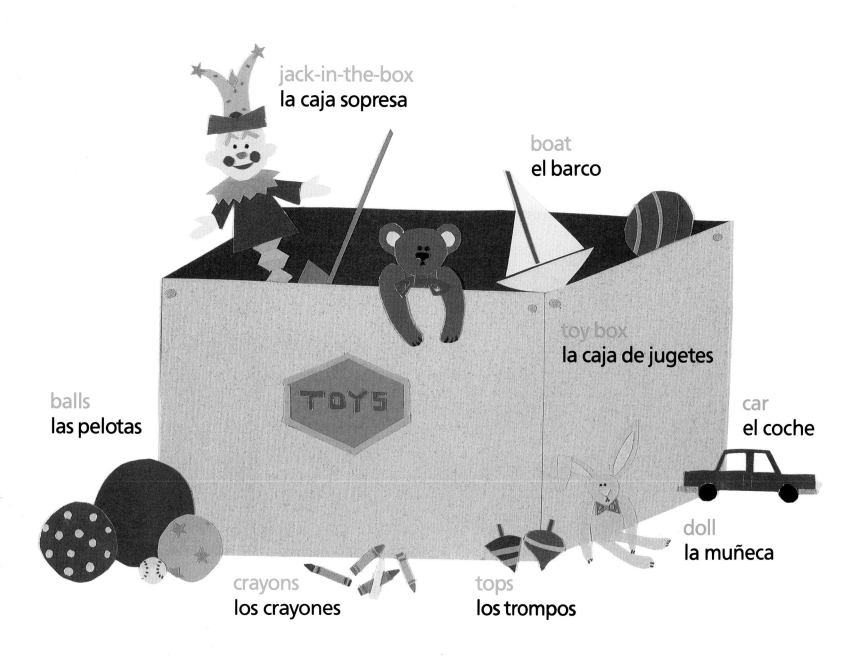

jack-in-the-box
la caja sopresa

boat
el barco

toy box
la caja de jugetes

balls
las pelotas

car
el coche

doll
la muñeca

crayons
los crayones

tops
los trompos

and these are my favorite toys.
y estos son mis jugetes favoritos.

window
la ventana

blocks
los bloques infantiles

mobile
el móvil

rocking chair
la mecedora

teddy bear
el osito de felpa

crib
la camita de nena

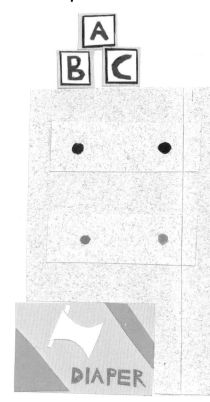

diapers
los pañales

This is my sister's room
Este es el cuarto de mi hermana

medicine cabinet
el botiquín

tissues
los pañuelitos

toilet paper
el papel higiénico

toilet
el excusado

shower
la ducha

faucet
la lĺave de agua

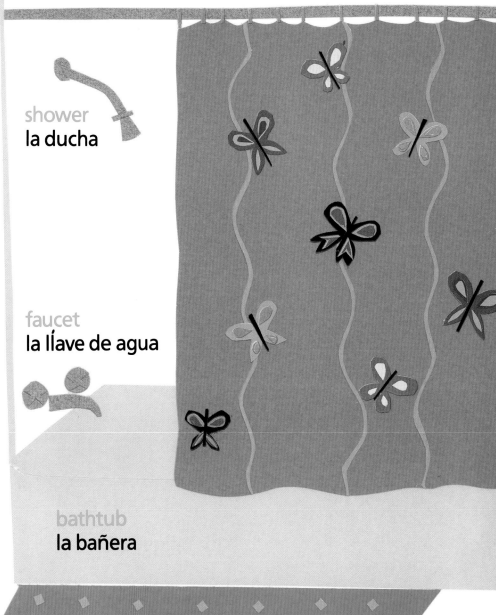

bathtub
la bañera

rug
la alfombra

and this is the bathroom.
y este es el baño.

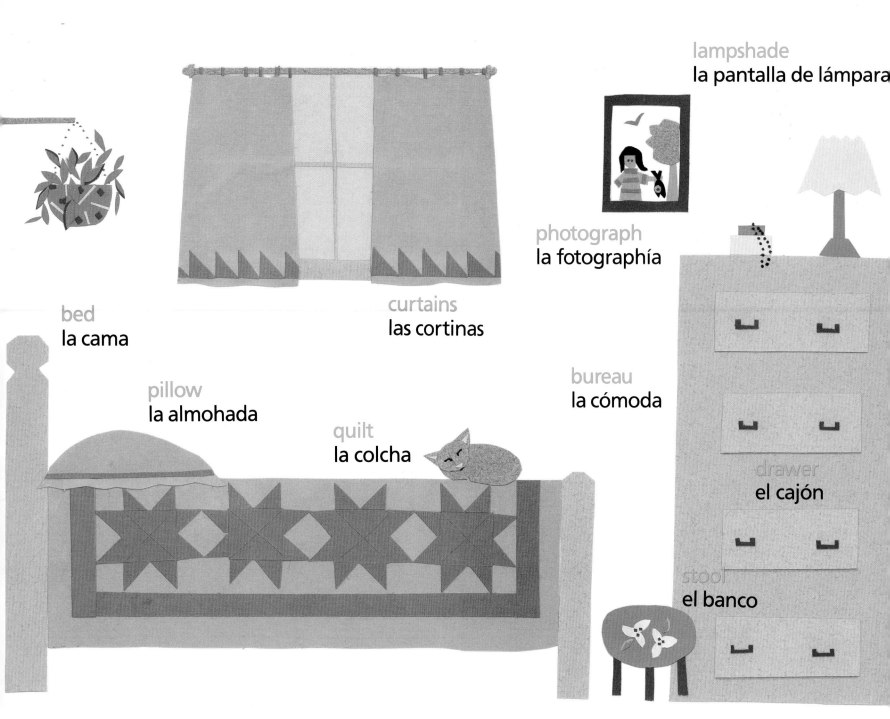

lampshade
la pantalla de lámpara

photograph
la fotographía

curtains
las cortinas

bed
la cama

bureau
la cómoda

pillow
la almohada

quilt
la colcha

drawer
el cajón

stool
el banco

This is my parents' bedroom.
Este es el cuarto de mis padres.

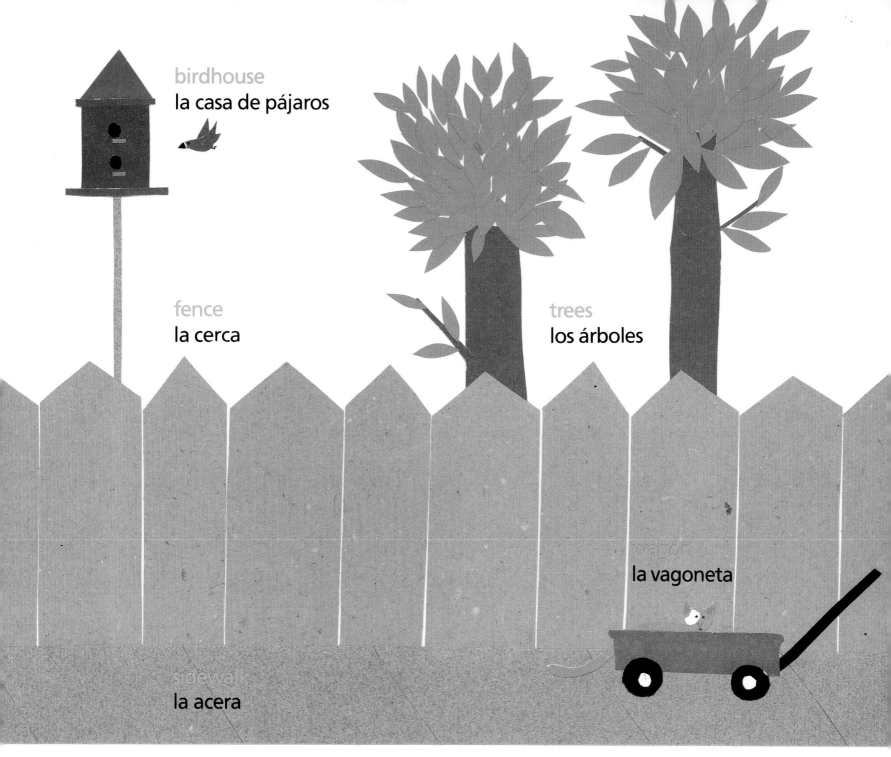

birdhouse
la casa de pájaros

trees
los árboles

fence
la cerca

wagon
la vagoneta

sidewalk
la acera

Let's go outside.
Salgamos.

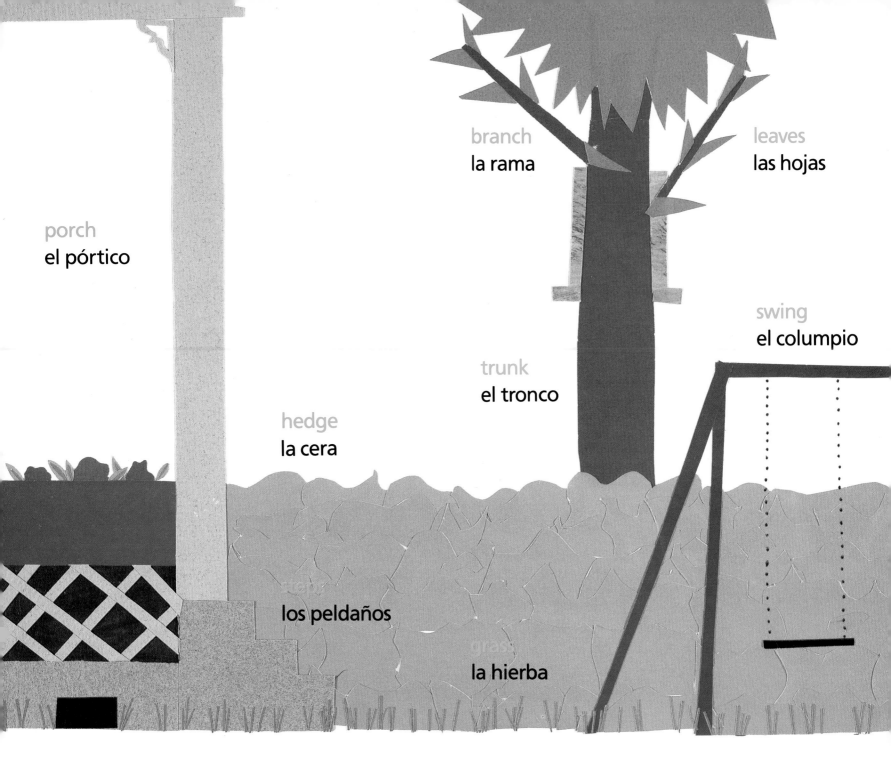

branch
la rama

leaves
las hojas

porch
el pórtico

swing
el columpio

trunk
el tronco

hedge
la cera

stairs
los peldaños

grass
la hierba

This is the yard.
Este es el patio.

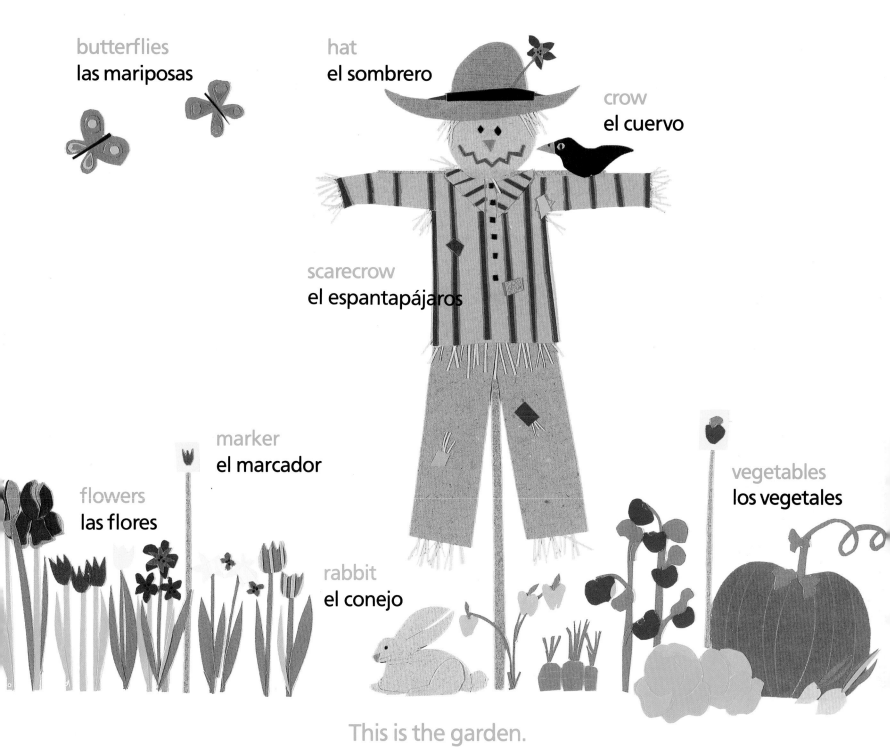

butterflies
las mariposas

hat
el sombrero

crow
el cuervo

scarecrow
el espantapájaros

marker
el marcador

flowers
las flores

vegetables
los vegetales

rabbit
el conejo

This is the garden.
Este es el jardín.

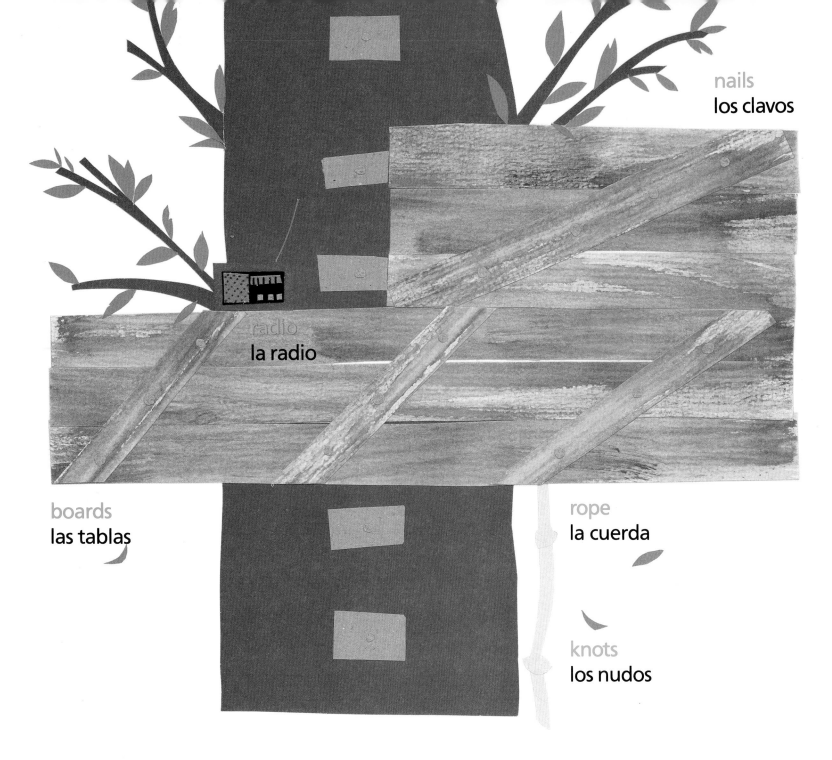

nails
los clavos

radio
la radio

boards
las tablas

rope
la cuerda

knots
los nudos

Let's go up to my treehouse.
Salgamos a mi casa del árbol

This is my house.
Esta es mi casa.

Some people live in igloos,
Algunas personas habitan en iglues,

or in tepees,
o en tipis,

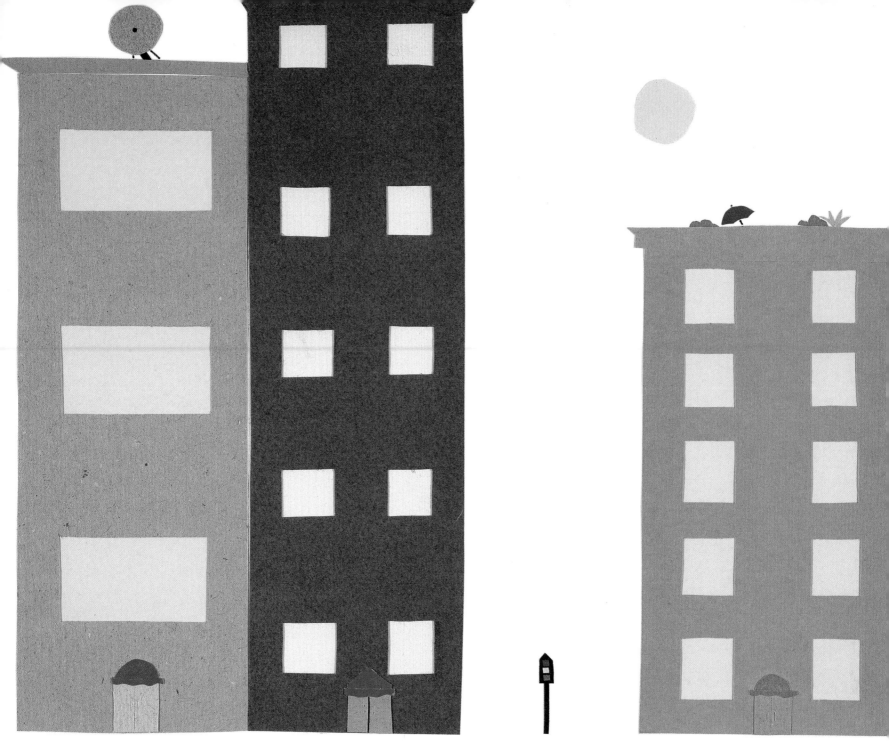

or in very tall apartment buildings.
o en edificios de apartamentos muy altos.

What kind of house do you live in?

¿En qué tipo de casa vives tú?